I'm Changing My Status

A SHIFT IN HOW WE SEE, THINK AND DO!

By

JAMES D. HOLIDAY SR.

Copyright © 2015 by Melchizedek Publishing

Book Cover Design: Tiffany Kameni.com

I'm Changing My Status by James D. Holiday, Sr.

ISBN 978-0-692-39941-5   1st print edition

All rights reserved. No part of this book may be reproduced, stored in a retrieval system, or transmitted in any form or by any means – electronic, mechanical, photocopy, recording, or any other—except for brief quotations in printed reviews, without the prior written consent of the publisher. If you purchase this book without a cover you should be aware that this book may have been stolen property and reported as "unsold and destroyed" to the Publisher. In such case neither the author nor the publisher has received any payment for this "stripped book."

Scripture quotations marked (KJV) are taken from the Holy Bible, Copyright © 1973, 1978, 1984 by Biblica, Inc. ™ Used by permission of Zondervan. All rights reserved worldwide. www.zondervan.com

DEDICATION

My wife Nicole A. Holiday has been such a motivating inspiration and I'd like to dedicate this book to her for she's given me two amazing sons (JD & NICK) and over 14 years of her life. It is because of her that I have pressed beyond many flaws, failures and challenges to become who I am today. My life is full of Favor because of her presence; I love and appreciate you "LADY!" I am privileged to Pastor an awesome company of believers at Word of Change Christian Fellowship, who have proven to be God sends in this season of my life. Thanks for all your support. I also want to thank Bishop Robert Anthony Anderson who is second to none when it comes to leadership and integrity. I salute you man of God and thank you for being a great Spiritual Father. To the King of Kings and the Lord of Lords saved me from a life of sin and chose me to be an Apostle to the nations. Father God I thank you for totally changing my status.

FOREWORD

Many people are frustrated in their lives because they can't put into words the feeling of exasperation, the feeling of hopelessness, or the feeling of utter desperation that seems to flood their minds on a daily basis. Pastor Holiday has captured the essence of the "stuck" mindset and masterfully put it into words. Poignant, clear instructions are given not only to get out of "neutral", but to shift your life into overdrive! Change Your Status causes you to take deep inventory of your life spiritually and naturally, and compels you to upgrade your current situation. No matter where you find yourself positionally in life, this book reveals that God has an even higher place reserved for you. Great read!

In His service,

Myron C. Meredith Jr.

King's Majesty Ministries, Pastor

"We Love You To Life!"

All throughout the bible God has sought a man to deliver His word and bring insight and direction to his people. Well God has done it again with a fresh voice for this season with a message that is designed to change your status. Pastor James D. Holiday Sr. takes us on a journey of spiritual growth, with his thought provoking and insightful writings.

He writes with purpose right from the start laying the foundation of elevation from the level you're on, all the way to mastering your season no matter where you find yourself today. His book speaks to the heart of the reader from a standpoint of been there, done that, no judgment nor condemnation. You sense that he has experienced and gained victory over the very things you are reading. Not only does he incorporate hard truth but he also allows God to speak prophetically throughout the pages.

The writing style of this book impacts the reader with decrees that your status is changing as if the same will that caused Pastor Holiday to overcome is now being activated in your life as you thumb through the pages. Pastor Holiday forces us into introspection where we have to face ourselves and the God we serve.

Who would have thought that satisfaction and comfort could cripple your momentum and progress? He blesses the reader with revelation knowledge end-to-end. A constant barrage of concentrated instructions that play out like slogans or jingles to help move you to Kingdom status. The author may or may not be known to you at this time but I believe Holy Spirit would want you to have this book in your library. I read it and "I'm Changing My Status" today!

Bishop Robert A. Anderson

Pastor of Empowerment Christian Center Church

Overseer of the E3 Fellowship of Churches

Introduction

I believe that these God inspired insights are going to challenge and bless your life. Open yourself up to be receptive to what God is saying in these pages while He gives you revelation and insight on the changes He's making in your life. You have every right to be in expectancy because of what's about to happen with your status.

TABLE OF CONTENTS

DEDICATION..3
FOREWORD..4
INTRODUCTION....................................7

Chapter 1: The Defining Moment..9

Chapter 2: Where Did I Go Wrong?...17

Chapter 3: Big Just Got Bigger..30

Chapter 4: God's Got Plans for You...39

Chapter 5: Making The Best Out of A Bad Situation....................................50

Chapter 6: Live Beyond The Shadow of Doubt..57

Chapter 7: Master Your Season............58

CHAPTER 1

THE "DEFINING" MOMENT

Whenever you transition from one level or place to another, something takes on a new status. Reason being is that there are necessary adjustments that have to be made in order to properly maintain, occupy and impact where you are now versus where you just left. I believe that one of the biggest struggles one can experience in life is embracing something totally new. Often times, when new concepts and methods are introduced to the life we think we've mastered, forward progress slows down or stops all because we are now trying to decide if we are going to embrace or reject the very thing that God has given us to enhance us. But let me encourage you right now when I say this, "Don't let what was, hinder what's coming!"

Change can only affect you based on how you view it, but when it comes to shifting from the OLD you to the NEW you; change is mandatory. Remaining the same is impossible after a true encounter with the God we serve. All throughout biblical history those that had encounters with Jesus left His presence with an upgraded status. He is in the business of Remodeling, Rehabilitating & Restructuring. He is in the business of upgrading lives. God delights in upgrading the lives of His People. I challenge you to prophesy to yourself and say "Self, It's time for an UPGRADE". There are some foundational things that are a must if you are going to upgrade and change your status.

(1) SEE THINGS SPIRITUALLY NOT SECULARLY

I Corinthians 2:14 The natural man receives not the things of God, for they are foolish unto him neither can he know them, because they are spiritually discerned.

(2) STAND ON THE SCRIPTURES

Isaiah 55:11 So shall my word be that goeth out of my mouth: it SHALL accomplish that which I please, and it shall prosper in the thing whereto I sent it.

(3) STEP OUT ON SURETY

I Corinthians 5:7 for we walk by faith not by sight. Faith comes from the (Greek word) Pis-Tis and it means Persuasion, belief and assurance.

Status = Position or rank in relation to others

This knowledge and revelation is key to the success of every believer because knowing what you are and who you are in Him fuels our ability to live a maximized life with minimal setbacks.

There are 3 different types of status

SOCIAL STATUS- Honor or prestige attached to ones position in society

ACHIEVED STATUS- Earned by your own ability and network of influence

ASCRIBED STATUS- Inherited positions, generally fixed for an individual at birth and/or through what they inherit.

It would be safe to say that regardless of how you achieve or obtain a type of status people use status as a way of measuring, labeling and categorizing. Status is always linked to one's measure or perception of worth & value, making it a "HOT" commodity. This is why we witness people sacrificing and compromising and ultimately losing themselves trying to get a particular status in life. We can look at what a person drives, wears and who they are in society to determine where they rank on society's status meter (or at least are trying to rank). I believe my assignment is not to knock, discredit or down play anyone's current status. Why? Because today's generation would call that hating on you, but as your prophetic and revelatory voice through this book, my assignment is to shift your thinking and mindset where you rank according to KINGDOM standards. It's all about Kingdom status and a prime example of that is found here in this text:

Psalms 8:5-6
⁵ Yet you made them only a little lower than God and crowned them with glory and honor.
⁶ You gave them charge of everything you made, putting all things under their authority—(Emphasis added)

We were made by God's design a little lower than the angels.

We were crowned with glory and honor.

We were made by God's design to have dominion (to rule or govern) over **EVERYTHING** He made and along with that God gave us authority also. Now that sounds like real status to me. The text says God made us to have dominion/God gave us authority, which validates that Kingdom status is neither ascribed nor achieved; it comes with your individual choice to allow God to both transition you and transform you into who He has destined for you to be. This is STATUS by design.

1 Peter 2:9 (KJV)
9 But ye are a chosen generation, a royal priesthood, an holy nation, a peculiar people; that ye should shew forth the praises of him who hath called you out of darkness into his marvelous light.

Chosen in this context means Selected, Picked, Elected, and Favored by God. Royal priesthood is a representation of God's elite core group. In essence we have been personally picked by God to be a part of His core group of elite (Kingdom) citizens, a peculiar people (set apart, unique, different). I feel led to tell you about yourself; because too many in the body of Christ are satisfied with their current status. This mindset is acceptable and common among believers simply because it doesn't challenge them to embrace anything different. You've reached a point in your life where it's a must that you lay some stuff to rest in your life. Why? Because your status has changed and it's not your fault that people are stuck in YOUR past and are clinging to YOUR history! It is not your responsibility to help people love who you have become, as it relates to your past with an individual or group of them. It's not your responsibility to help deliver people from what you have already let go. Please understand that during this shift there will be those in your life that are still where you were and are determined to stay where you used to be. That's fine for them, but you are not obligated to that place any longer because there has been an upgrade in your status.

For some people whatever direction the wind blows, that's the direction they are headed in, not because they want or are forced to, but simply because of their inability to distinguish between who they are and who they are trying to be. If there was ever a time to be sure about who you are as a person in God is now. There is so much going on in this life that manifesting your true identity in God can be lost or misinterpreted. If you don't know who you are, you'll journey down the wrong path continuously, because who you are and where you are headed must line up. Quality decisions and godly choices will get you there, but character keeps you there. God has revealed to me that identity is **WHO** you are and image is **HOW** you are. This is a time where people couldn't careless if they gained access to the deep things of God, but are just content with being accepted, liked and received by people. Now what they become is directly linked to who they are associated with and connected to. Many who have failed to make the status upgrade hide behind titles, associations, affiliations, memberships, clubs and organizations. I've discovered that even in cases like this, most of the time those associations are worse off collectively than you are individually. Don't lose yourself before you find yourself.

In I Peter 2:9, Apostle Peter clarifies that our Father never intended for us to struggle with identity issues. In **verse 9,** it deals with the Father's excellence of choice and elements of our character. <u>*V9 but ye are a chosen generation, a royal priesthood, an holy nation, a peculiar people; that ye should shew forth the praises of him who hath called you out of darkness into his marvelous light.*</u>

It is a must that the people of God stop selling their souls to the highest bidder. We are precious to the Father and you must determine within yourself that you're not going to be satisfied with a pawn shop appraisal of yourself any longer. You are peculiar (set apart, different) which makes it safe to say "so what you're different, it's supposed to be that way!" When you cannot identify who you are, you become a slave to everybody else's opinion of you. **Matthew 5:13-14** says we are the salt of the earth and the light of the world therefore validating the fact that we as believers can affect our atmosphere. You set the bar; you raise the standard because we are the trend setters, pioneers and trail blazers of this day and time. Stop letting others cause you to contradict your confidence, because people who have not made the upgrade with you will sometimes mistake your assurance for arrogance and your passion for aggression. I declare today that it is no longer your problem that people can't handle you knowing your Kingdom place and privileges. Can I encourage you to let people come up to where you are and don't go down to where they are. Often times the lives we live are a result of an individual being more comfortable acting like what people say they are rather than what God says they are. Of course when the façade doesn't work out, they don't take responsibility for it and blame others. When this becomes the norm, you'll find yourself somewhere in the middle neither hot or cold.

Chapter 2
Where Did I Go Wrong?

I want to shed some light on how God feels concerning His relationship with His People. Anybody that has ever been loved or in love before, can attest to the fact that you know when things are not the same. Nothing has to be said, reviewed, discussed or even mentioned; you just know things are different. Don't get me wrong, things are still getting done; time is still being spent, efforts still being made but no enthusiasm in the efforts. Things that used to be done with a smile are now done with a frown. It used to be high priority now it's irrelevant. Things that stayed on your mind somehow slips your mind now. Change for the worse begins to creep in totally unaware, but since there is consistency in the routine you don't doubt the persons love for you. But based on visible proof and concrete evidence, you can clearly say that person doesn't love you like they used to. For example:

<u>Date nights are less frequent</u>

<u>Intimate time is rare</u>

<u>Quality time is every now and then</u>

<u>Gratitude is hardly expressed</u>

<u>Compliments cease</u>

Hot is now cold and you are hardly ever motivated to keep the love alive, therefore as a result, the relationship has taken a major shift in your love walk. I am certain that you can relate to what I am saying, because you've at some point experienced or experiencing it now. I must be real with you today when I tell you this, what I am referring to has absolutely nothing to do with your relationship with your man, wife, husband or woman. I am talking specifically about the detour that many have made in their relationship with the Father. Most of what I've mentioned that you thought was building a strong case against your spouse or better half, was really helping the Father build a strong case against YOU. Why? Because based on what you've been giving Him lately, He has the right to say that you don't love Him like you used to.

Revelation 2:4-5

4. "But I have this complaint against you. You don't love me or each other as you did at first! 5. Look how far you have fallen! Turn back to me and do the works you did at first. If you don't repent, I will come and remove your lampstand from its place among the churches. **(Emphasis added)**

Here in this text, Jesus Himself is speaking and if I could express my interpretation, what He's saying is "I'm not feeling this!" If you and I are not going to accept things being any kind of way, then what makes you think that He will? Especially if that's not how you used to be with Him. In Revelation Chapter 2, the churches had retained its purity of doctrine and worship, but were lacking deep devotion to the Father. Sounds like TODAY? In upgrading your status and making a Kingdom shift, you must realize that routine service and duty are not enough. Just going through the motions is not enough and playing your role at church isn't going to cut it either.

Romans 12:1 (KJV) *I beseech you therefore, brethren, by the mercies of God, that ye present your bodies a living sacrifice, holy, acceptable unto God, which is your reasonable service.*

There must be an upgrade in your overall lifestyle. You must see your life as a presentation to God. In order to be a living sacrifice (a living person whose flesh has died to sin), we must die to ourselves in order to offer ourselves as a gift to God that is HOLY & ACCEPTABLE!

Revelation 3:15-16
15 "I know all the things you do, that you are neither hot nor cold. I wish that you were one or the other!
16 But since you are like lukewarm water, neither hot nor cold, I will spit you out of my mouth!

You know you don't love God like you used to when you find yourself somewhere in the middle, you haven't given up but you're not all in either. I can hear God saying: "What happened to what you use to give Me? What happened to the old you? In Revelations 3:16, God is saying that He wants all of you or none of you at all! This is what God is saying concerning your lukewarm relationship with Him.

You used to try to get to know me through
(PERSONAL STUDY)

You used to talk to me in **(PRAYER)**

You used to compliment me in **(WORSHIP)**

You used to celebrate me through **(PRAISE)**

You used to support me by
(SOWING SEEDS AND GIVING)

You used to spend time with me during
(MEDITATION)

I CAN HEAR GOD SAYING:

You don't take me anywhere by
(WITNESSING)

You don't represent me any more with your
(CONDUCT)

You don't fear & respect me any more through
(OBEDIENCE)

Apostle Paul told the Galatian church in Chapter 5 verse 7 of his letter to them, "You were doing good, but what has interfered with you to hold you back from following what is right?"

Psalm 119:9 *How shall a young man cleanse his way? By taking heed and keeping watch [on himself] according to your word [conforming his life to it]. (Emphasis added)*

The word **Cleanse** in its original context means "to be translucent, make clean, and counted as pure." The phrase **Take Heed** means to "make a hedge about, guard, and give attention to. We have got to get to circumspect living if we are going to have success as believers.

CIRCUMSPECT-CAREFULLY CONSIDER ALL CIRCUMSTANCES AND CONSEQUENCES :

Steps To Becoming Circumspect

1. Don't ignore what you need to deal with!
2. Take ownership!
3. Reputation should not make you renege on what is right.

ROMANS 7:19-*21* *I FAIL TO PRATICE THE GOOD THINGS I WANT TO DO, BUT THE THINGS I DO NOT WANT TO DO, IM ALWAYS DOING. EVERY TIME I SET MY MIND TO DO GOOD, EVIL IS ALWAYS READILY AVAILABLE. (Emphasis Added)*

Getting this thing right, CAN NOT be done on your own. We must walk in a:

1. GREATER WISDOM

Galatians 5:25 If we live in the Spirit, let us also walk in the Spirit.

2. GREATER AUTHORITY

Philippians 4:13 I have strength for all things in Christ Who empowers me [I am ready for anything and equal to anything through Him who infuses inner strength into me; I am self-sufficient in Christ's sufficiency]. (Emphasis added)

3. GREATER POWER

Luke 10:19 Behold! I have given you authority and power to trample upon serpents and scorpions, and [physical and mental strength and ability] over all the power that the enemy [possesses]; and nothing shall in any way harm you. (Emphasis added)

The Father has equipped us with spiritual resources that exceed the tempting influences around us. This strength, wisdom and authority

is found and obtained through reading GODS WORD and DOING WHAT IT SAYS!
The word must move from the pages of a book to the pages of our LIFE!

Psalm 119:10-11 KJV
With my whole heart have I sought thee: O let me not wander from thy commandments. Thy word have I hid in mine heart that I might not sin against thee.

3 SELF CHECK QUESTIONS

1. HOW CAN GOD TRULY BLESS YOU IF YOU ARE CONSTANTLY PUTTING HIM IN POSITION WHERE HE HAS TO PUNISH YOU?

2. HOW CAN GOD DELIVER YOU IF YOU DESIRE WHAT YOU DONT NEED MORE THAN WHAT HE IS OFFERING?

3. HOW CAN GOD SET YOU FREE WHEN, WHO AND WHAT HAS YOU BOUND IS MORE SIGNIFICANT THAN GOD?

Compromised priorities will always produce uncompromising positions. Whenever you find yourself in a position where you are making a decision you don't want to make, it is the result of not making the decision you should have made initially. There is a difference between a choice and a decision! Choices generally are a guess based on what you hope the outcome to be or become. Decisions are selections made based on the weighing of pros and cons of a given situation. Choices are made with right now in mind! Decisions are made with the future in mind!

Proverbs 16:3
Roll your works upon the Lord [commit and trust them wholly to Him; He will cause your thoughts to become agreeable to His will, and] so shall your plans be established and succeed. (Emphasis added)

COMMIT WHAT YOU DO TO THE LORD AND YOUR PLANS WILL SUCCEED!

Just when you think you have it ALL figured out, here comes another question to answer, problem to solve or dilemma to face. I would dare say that life produces the heaviest weights we will ever have to lift. You give your time, talent, treasure only to feel as if all you got left to give is "UP". You tried everything from switching jobs, changing churches, and changing hairstyles but none of those things help. You start getting into the Word and improving your prayer life, things are looking up; but for some strange reason what you have isn't fulfilling or what you really want in life. If you are going to have and experience better, you "MUST" realize that how you feel can no longer be the GPS that gives direction to the course of your life.

You must get in tune with your feelings so you won't become overly influenced by them. You must be conscious of your feelings so you won't become consumed by them. This is all done by constantly checking your feelings with the WORD of God

Galatians 5:25
If we live by the [Holy] Spirit, let us also walk by the Spirit. [If by the Holy Spirit we have our life in God, let us go forward walking in line, our conduct controlled by the Spirit.] (Emphasis added)

Why? Because the Father doesn't deal with our feelings. (Soulish realm, Will, Emotions etc.) He deals with us directly through the spirit.
He won't invest Kingdom resources in something that a man can control. Everything from the Kingdom stays under kingdom dominion. He speaks and deals with our Spirit Man. Which if we are Kingdom connected, we should be under his control operating under Kingdom authority. You've missed enough mighty moves of God, favor, blessings, and answered prayers using the wrong formula; don't forfeit the favor of your future all because doing

you is more than important than pleasing God. "It is not that serious!"

I CORINTHIANS 10:31 *Whatsoever ye do, do ALL to the glory of GOD!*

II TIMOTHY 2:21 *If a man therefore purge himself from these, he shall be a vessel unto honour, sanctified, and meet for the master's use, and prepared unto every good work."*

This scripture means that if you keep yourself pure, you will be an instrument God can use for His Purpose. Your Life will be clean and you will be ready for the master to use you for every good work.

Raggedy lives produce raggedy results! Pure lives produce power! I feel led to tell you today, that your struggles in life comes as a result of your lifestyle. Your lifestyle is a direct result of your "life's" style. God will not promote, favor or bless what He doesn't endorse! What we are up against in this day and time, I have come to believe the answer is not in our heads but it is in the Spirit.

EPHESIANS 6:*12 For we wrestle not against flesh and blood, but against principalities, powers, and rulers of darkness of this world* *and against spiritual wickedness in high places.*

I believe that's what Paul told us in **Colossians 3:2** to "**set your affections on things above, not on things on the earth.**"

He knew that a Kingdom mindset would keep us in proper posture to receive and release in the earth realm. There is a level in God that the people of God have yet to attain that has keys and resources that are vital to spiritual success on this level. There are three things that are a must if you plan on experiencing God on the level He intended for every believer.

1. **SIGNIFICANCE IN YOUR SEEKING** - *Matthew 6:33*
   Seek the Kingdom of God above all else, and live righteously, and he will give you everything you need. (Emphasis added)

2. **SINCERITY IN YOUR SERVICE** - *Colossians 3:23 (KJV) And whatsoever ye do, do it heartily, as to the Lord, and not unto men;*

3. **SUBSTANCE IN YOUR SOWING** - *Proverbs 3:9*

Honor the LORD with your wealth and with the best parts of everything you produce. (Emphasis added)

We as believers must be willing to embrace wholeheartedly the things that God requires of us if we are going to experience His fullness. The choice is **ALL** yours. All your excuses were nailed to the cross. To go after this, one must understand that God's plan is perfect, precise and progressive. When you work His Plan; you prosper in all areas of life and prosperity is not limited to finances, but covers the whole man in its entirety including health, wealth, mind, and ministry, etc. There has to be an elevation of how we view the potential of our sacrifices. Why? Because often times, sacrifices are not made because they involve giving up something, someone or somewhere in the process. Please understand the sacrifices you make for the Father have a flip side as well, called reward and promise. If you are willing to take a step in God's direction, you will find yourself overcoming the challenges that you have mastered all your life. You will be surprised at the doors that are waiting on you to walk through them.

Chapter 3
BIG JUST GOT BIGGER

Regardless to who you are and what you have, their will come a time in your life where there will be no more covers to hide under. Whether now or later you will have to come clean and face your failures, shortcomings and sin. You're living the life you live because you're really trying to cover up the life you don't like. You've had that 1 on 1 with the mirror and he told you a thing or two about yourself, forcing you to magnify what you have fought for years to minimize. Sin has been around a long time and since the beginning of time, people have been coming up short in living a life free from sin. So let me encourage you when I say this; you are not the first person to mess some stuff up in their life, habitually miss the mark or come up short. Stop penalizing yourself personally because that will paralyze you spiritually. Often times people fall victim to the judgments, opinions and views of everybody else, but fail to realize that what "they" say, feel and think is totally irrelevant when it comes to the Father's view of their current position in life.

Man judges but the Father says:
Isaiah 1:18
¹⁸ "Come now, let's settle this," says the LORD. "Though your sins are like scarlet, I will make them as white as snow. Though they are red like crimson, I will make them as white as wool. (Emphasis added)

Man condemns but the Father's says:
1 John 1:9 (KJV)
⁹ If we confess our sins, he is faithful and just to forgive us *our* sins, and to cleanse us from all unrighteousness.

Stop being skeptical and sensitive because you're worried about people and their input. Get your mind right and your emotions together and do you in Christ, because EVERYBODY is an EX- something!

Romans 3:23 tells us that ALL have sinned and come short of the glory of God.
"All" comes from the Greek word **Paus** which means "everyone, no exceptions, picks or chooses". Even on your best day, minus grace and mercy, we all are equivalent to filthy rags. Even as a Pastor, what gets under my skin is people who forget the fact that everybody is guilty of something but walk around like they are Judge Mathis or a prosecutor treating you like a criminal in their little court of law. You are being

judged and accused by others like they have no flaws and have a squeaky clean background.

Luke 6:37
³⁷ "Do not judge others, and you will not be judged. Do not condemn others, or it will all come back against you. Forgive others, and you will be forgiven. (Emphasis added)

Some of the deepest hurt believers go through and experience comes from other believers. Lots of people stop going to church, won't go to church and even hate the church because of somebody in the church planting detrimental seeds that have taken root and produced something in the person that now requires deliverance. If you can go anywhere to get peace, encouragement, inspiration and direction, it should be the church. Some people never get that because their attention is being redirected to bad attitudes, rolling eyes, funky dispositions and cliques who have church down to a science but their life is a complete mess. My goal in this chapter is to help you out of that oppressing shell of a life into a liberating life where you are confident and understanding of your worth in God for He loves you just the way you are. Let today be the day that you stop feeling inferior, insignificant and intimidated by people who are flawed just like you. Take your rightful place in God, walk in a new life of confidence and assurance in who you are not who you used to be.

2 Corinthians 5:17 (KJV)
¹⁷ Therefore if any man be in Christ, he is a new creature: old things are passed away; behold all things are become new.

No matter who or what they are in ministry, everybody has failed and disappointed God before. But you have got to be man or woman enough to acknowledge that sin is your problem not everyone else. Many confess sin but never give it up completely, which leads to a reputation of repeating the same or similar acts. Sin applies to us all, because no person alive is without it in some way shape form or fashion. We must realize four key things about sin.

1. **SIN STINKS IN GOD'S NOSTRILS**
2. **SIN STUNTS OUR SPIRITUAL GROWTH**
3. **SIN STOPS US FROM BEING BLESSED**
4. **SIN SEPERATES US FROM THE FATHER**

<u>**Always remember!**</u>

Romans 6:23 (KJV)
²³ For the wages of sin is death; but the gift of God is eternal life through Jesus Christ our Lord.

If you keep it real with yourself, you can honestly admit that you should be at a place in your life where there are just certain things you just avoid, certain people you don't associate with and specific places you don't go anymore. This choice is not made because you have arrived or a big shot who's better than anybody, but simply because you are on a different page in your life now. You must embrace the fact that freedom is a choice and because of the very nature of God being present in our lives, we have a divine right to live freely in God without any hindrances or restrictions from anyone or anything. No person place or things has the authorization or ability to keep you bound, hindered or restricted. Who and what you are linked to is based on your desires and perception. Your connection to God is based on the presence of the **HOLY SPIRIT** who gives you the ability to walk in total liberation from bondage to liberty.

2 Corinthians 3:17 (KJV)
¹⁷ Now the Lord is that Spirit: and where the Spirit of the Lord is, there is liberty.

Getting free is not always the struggle for some people.

A lot of people can:
Break loose and let go!
Break free and give it up!
Break out and stop!
Break away and come clean!

But when it comes to staying free and delivered, that's when the heat and pressure turns up which is where people return back to the very place they were delivered and free from. We start rehearsing bad memories, contrary thoughts, bad relationships and feeling incomplete again. You start connecting back to people who used, abused and disrespected you in the past. The pressures of life if not careful, can cause you to run back to the same bondage and oppression that kept you broken, hating and disgusted with yourself. I can remember being at that place myself, it almost drove me crazy, crushed my heart, broke my spirit and altered my life. I've learned that when you've experienced and overcome certain things in life, you get one up on the enemy.

What Life Has Taught Me:

(1) Experience is an excellent teacher.
(2) Experience is a prescription for prevention.
(3) Experience causes you to recognize things beforehand.
(4) Experience affords you a sneak preview of potential pitfalls.

Galatians 5:1 (KJV)
¹ Stand fast therefore in the liberty wherewith Christ hath made us free, and be not entangled again with the yoke of bondage.

Getting free is easy but staying free is where the fight begins. When you get free, there are 3 things that must be done which is: **(1) Recognize who set you free-** John 8:36 It says whoever the son sets free is free indeed (ABSOLUTELY FREE This verse validates that when the Lord does it, consider it done. **(2) Respond to what He did-** James 4:7 says submit yourself to God, resist the devil and he will flee from you. **(3) Remain-**The B clause of Galatians 5:1 says be not entangled again with the yoke of bondage. Let me help you when I say this, you've seen, heard and done it before, what makes you think the outcomes going to be any different than before?

2 Corinthians 5:17 (KJV)
17 Therefore if any man be in Christ, he is a new creature: old things are passed away; behold all things are become new.

When you are changing your status, you have got to get to the point where the new you is not attracted to old stuff anymore. A changed status will cause you to stare the residue of your past dead in the face and not even think about breathing life back into it. When you're headed toward destiny, you are no longer a slave to history. I challenge you to change how you embrace decision making, **before you answer, be sure to analyze, before you indulge, be sure to investigate, before you get involved be sure to get an understanding**. I am surprised at the number of people who play dumb because of curiosity, it sounds, looks and seems good but you know for a fact that you have been down that path too often. The secret to changing your status permanently and staying free is, you must love God more than anything or anybody in this whole world! You can't go back! Why? Because you barely made it out last time. You might not get another chance, another turn or another opportunity; it may not be a next time if you go back. I encourage you to stay free! As a matter of fact, prophecy to yourself right now; and say **"I Will Stay Free"**! You worked too hard to get where you are to go back. Set your mind that you will make every struggle, tear, hard time and obstacle count from here on out. You paid a hefty tab for your testimony, don't pawn it for another opportunity to give your flesh what it's asking for. Your Big just got Bigger!

Chapter 4
GOD'S GOT PLANS FOR YOU

It's one thing to make plans for yourself or someone else, but there is a certain level of excitement and anticipation that you feel when someone makes plans for you. There are 5 things you want to know when this occurs: WHO made plans? WHAT plans where made? WHEN are the plans for? WHERE are the plans? & WHY were the plans made? Plans give you a reason to look beyond your present state. Along with your status, your mindset must shift to knowing that what you are tolerating is only temporary especially when you are dealing with people places and situations in life. Plans give you something to go after and make preparations for. Life is not something we should be living for the moment never planning anything. Things come out better when you make plans because there is no aimless searching and just existing. Plans keep you consistent and focused on making sure nobody or nothing interfere with those plans.

It is something, to know that outside of all the family functions and social gatherings that lace our calendar, we serve a BIG GOD who is responsible for everything and everyone but is never too busy to make plans for us. Where you are in life, what you are involved in, dealing with and going through in your life RIGHT NOW doesn't have the ability to cancel God's ultimate plan for your life. Being willing to shift mentally has everything to do with God's ultimate plan for your life. You may have a generic off brand perception of yourself all because your plans in life have failed and this has caused you to link your flawed past with a failed present to God's future plans. I take authority NOW!! Even as I am typing this section I feel the presence of God, I bind the spirit of failure and defeat and I break its grip off of your life. You will not be stuck in this place any longer. I challenge you to measure your progress from where you started and not where you are, understanding that the plan of God for your life trumps any other plan for your life, even your own. Prophesy to yourself RIGHT NOW: THE PLAN OF GOD TRUMPS EVERY OTHER PLAN FOR MY LIFE!

Jeremiah 29:11 (KJV)
¹¹ For I know the thoughts that I think toward you, saith the LORD, thoughts of peace, and not of evil, to give you an expected end.

Let me encourage you when I say this; what you messed up, where you failed and how you came up short has nothing to do with the fact that God has bigger and better plans for your future. Stop trying to figure out your future and just focus on obeying. Stay in tune with your now because the wrong focus can cause failure, especially if it's on the wrong people, place and things. **You're so focused on what's about to happen that you miss what is happening. You're so focused on what's getting ready to change that you miss what has changed. You're so focused on what might work that you lose sight of what is working.** Before you can ever embrace destiny, you must erase distractions. I promise you that God has plans for you. Now that we understand that, I want to warn you that even though nothing can stop God's ultimate plan for your life; deliberate dis-obedience can definitely delay it.

EXAMPLES

1. You know what the word says concerning that life but you do it any way.

2. You know what God has told you to do, but you do your own thing.

3. It's been prophesied, spoken over your life, revealed and confirmed but you reject it.

4. You've dreamed it, felt it, and experienced it but deliberately detour from the direction God wants you to head in, all because of your own plans.

That is why it won't work! That is why it won't last! That is why it won't come together, because you cannot implement carnal principles into a spiritual plan.

God is specific with His instructions, which makes it very obvious when we go against His will for our lives. **Jeremiah 1:5 says that before you were even formed in your mother's womb, God knew you and sanctified you and ordained you a prophet.** It is biblically safe to say that God was making plans for you before you even got here, so what makes you think a few human errors, mistakes or flaws can destroy what God was planning for you before your existence. You and the Father are not the only two with plans for your life; Satan has plans also. **Luke 22:31 says that Satan has a desire to have you, that he might sift you as wheat. John 10:10 says that the thief comes (WITH A PLAN) to kill, steal and destroy.** In **Jeremiah 29,** we see God getting a word to His people even though they are in a situation. In **verses 1-9,** God confirmed that He saw the state they were in, in fact He knew all about it because He was the one who put them there. You will always find yourself in a situation when you make alternate plans. **Verse 10** of that same chapter, God tells His people through His prophet that they would be in their situation 70 years, but He would soon come and change their status by bringing them home. Every now and then you will find yourself in a particular state for an extended period of time, but it does not determine how and when God moves. Just be confident that He's going to keep His commitment to those who He loves. The 70 years of judgment was God's plan to prompt His people to seek Him wholeheartedly like they had before. Once they turned back to God, He would gather them from their place of bondage. All I am trying to say is no matter where you are in life, how long you have been there; God still has a plan for you. I know it has been a long time. I know it has been inconsistent, cloudy, and crazy lately, but thanks be to God that gives us the victory through Christ Jesus. There are plans to look forward to like in **Psalm 84:11 that says, God is a sun and shield He gives grace and glory and no good thing will He withhold from them that WALK UPRIGHTLY.** Now this should encourage you to get excited about your future! The uncommon always seems too uncomfortable. Why? Because it stretches us and it's my opinion that if we are going to grow and expand in different areas of our lives we will have to do some stretching. What you are about walk into is going to need some more room. The worst thing you can do is come into a season that you have not made preparations to accommodate what comes with it. You have to start making preparations beforehand mentally, physically, emotionally and spiritually. Whatever it is that is occupying space in those areas need to be inventoried and properly accessed, because old and new don't always mix no matter how careful and strategic you are. With change comes an area of the unknown that forces you to trust beyond your own abilities and strengths. Guess what? That's right where God wants you, trusting beyond your own abilities and strengths. ***Proverbs 3:5 Tells us to trust in the Lord with ALL your heart and lean not to our own understanding, acknowledge Him in ALL your ways and He will direct your path***. A bright future starts with a path that is properly directed. God has to be the pilot, quarterback and driver because a life in Him requires you to follow His pre-ordained destination for you. I am excited for you and firmly believe that you want something bigger, better and greater from God. A simple revelation I want to drop on you before moving forward and that is "Getting, starts with wanting". Desire is the fuel of destiny, so I challenge you to fill up on desire today and let it ignite a fire in you that will burn hot until you reach that place in God that was tailor made for you and your purpose. I prophesy **SUCCESS** over your life through the pages of this book and pray that you get very uncomfortable being typical, average and ordinary. I declare that you are not next, you are now! What you are waiting on is waiting on you! Go get your life back and line it up with the path headed in God's direction and not yours. I say to you that "I will not except another excuse from you as to why you can't, didn't or couldn't!" **YOU ARE NOT NEXT, YOU ARE NOW!**

As we approach certain dates on the calendar such as holidays, birthdays and anniversaries; regardless to what's going on in our lives at that time, there is still a level of excitement that we feel as those days approach us. Life seems more livable when there is something to look forward to. Especially when what you are looking forward to is better than what you currently have, had or are experiencing right now. Nothing is more gratifying and fulfilling then when what you are anticipating becomes a reality. What is to come becomes your right now, your future becomes your present and your current becomes destiny. On the flip side, it is sad when you live your life never expecting, wishing or hoping for anything. It is really sad when you never look beyond right now, always living for the moment. But let me shock your system with this statement, "RIGHT NOW IS NOT FOREVER." I have discovered something pastoring God's people and ministering around the United States that not only do people need deliverance from their past, but they also need deliverance from their present (RIGHT NOW). A lot of believers are fine right where they are at, with who they got and what they got. Some of God's women have been baby mommas, girlfriends, significant others and dip offs so long that becoming a wife doesn't even cross their mind. Some of God's men have been boyfriends, baby daddies, sugar daddies and friend with benefits so long, that becoming a husband doesn't every enter their thoughts. Don't get me wrong, I totally understand the fact that some things take time and strategic steps, but just because you may be in a situation don't mean you have to be satisfied in it. Satisfaction breeds comfort and comfort is paralyzing and crippling people when it comes to progression and momentum in the things of God. I activate Philippians 4:13 in your life that you can do all things through Christ that strengthens you. Often times we are our own worst enemy when it comes to the fate of our future and destiny. Beloved, God is to be obeyed and not understood. Don't allow yourself to not to keep yourself from going. Remember Abram in Genesis chapter 12, the Lord told him to leave his comfort zone along with those who he was connected to and familiar with. He was instructed to go to an undisclosed destination. Sometimes where you are headed has to become irrelevant when it comes to extreme obedience to the Father. Sometimes, you just have to go even when you don't know, trusting GOD with your whole heart looks foolish to people who are not spiritual, so be careful who you listen to and confer with when it comes to your future, because all it takes is one word to cause interference with the voice of God and now you've detoured from the path trying to take an alternate route to where God is sending you. I want to encourage you with three simple suggestions, that I feel will bless you.

1. **STOP GIVING TEMPORARY THINGS PERMANENT ATTENTION**

2. **STOP GIVING TEMPORARY PEOPLE PERMANENT TIME**

3. **STOP GIVING TEMPORARY PLACES A PERMANENT TOUCH**

Why? Because if you are truly changing your status, you will need the rest of you for the best of you. The day you stop striving is the day you become a slave to your situation. STOP complaining and start conquering. STOP doubting and start believing. STOP making excuses and start making moves. I dare you to get actively involved in the outcome of your future by putting yourself in position to actually receive instruction from God. I speak victory over your life and by the power of the Holy Ghost I cancel your pity party subscription in the name of Jesus. Please know and embrace the fact that what is coming is better than what has been and far better than what is. I think it's time you cried your last tear, let it all go and pick yourself back up again getting excited about your future. You have every right to get excited about your future because how it is now is not how it's going to stay. Apostle Paul says in Philippians 3:13 forget those things which are behind, press toward the mark for the prize of the high calling..... Many have stopped and refuse to press because they have taken their eyes off the prize. Focus is essential to your growth, elevation and change. The more you focus on what is to come, the more excited you get about how things are going to turn out in your life. I can deal with a horrible today, as long as I know I have a hopeful tomorrow. I Corinthians 2:9, Apostle Paul makes a clear declaration that what you are in store for is far better than what you are involved in. He says "as it is written eyes hath not seen, neither ear heard, neither have it entered the heart of man...." He was referring specifically to the very things that God himself has custom designed and tailor made to fit your life. You are in better shape than you think and the enemy is not fighting you because of your now but his attack is predicated on where you are headed. I promise you that right now is not forever! I speak directly to you reading this book right now; you have messed around and put God in a position where He has to bless you. You've been faithful, serving, sowing and sacrificing and I can say that with assurance because His word declares that He is a rewarder of them that diligently seek Him. Psalm 84:11b says "no good thing will he withhold from them that walk uprightly". I thank God for your future, because it looks better than your past and present. Be encouraged man or woman of God, I decree that your status is changing even as you are reading these prophetic pages of this book. On your mark, get set, GO!!!!!

Chapter 5
MAKING THE BEST OUT OF A BAD SITUATION

I've discovered that a condition whether mental, emotional, spiritual or physical; it will cause you to do one of two things which is accept it or do something about it. Regardless to who you are or what you have accomplished, everyone has issues they need addressing and problems they need solving. Some people's conditions are more obvious than others some are exposed or hidden but whatever the case is, we recognize that it's there and not going anywhere. I would dare to say that many issues have longevity simply because the Lord is the only one with the ULTIMATE cure.

You've dealt with it so long until it has almost become second nature and just a part of life as you know it. Let me remind you by way of John 10:10b that Jesus, Our Lord and Savior declares that He came that we might have life more abundantly. So if your condition consumes you to a point where life is not enjoyable, liberated and drama free then it is safe to say that you are not living the life God has ordained for you. This simple truth that I have brought to focus with my last few statements makes it safe to say that it is time to **CHANGE YOUR STATUS**. It doesn't matter how good your job pays, how compatible you and your better half are or how supportive your circle is. When the smoke clears, reality sets in and you are forced to acknowledge the person in the mirror; it is still you and your condition still remains.

Mark 10:47-52 (KJV)

47 And when he heard that it was Jesus of Nazareth, he began to cry out, and say, Jesus, thou Son of David, have mercy on me.

48 And many charged him that he should hold his peace: but he cried the more a great deal, Thou Son of David, have mercy on me.

49 And Jesus stood still, and commanded him to be called. And they call the blind man, saying unto him, be of good comfort, rise; he calleth thee.

50 And he, casting away his garment, rose, and came to Jesus.

51 And Jesus answered and said unto him, what wilt thou that I should do unto thee? The blind man said unto him, Lord, that I might receive my sight.

52 And Jesus said unto him, Go thy way; thy faith hath made thee whole. And immediately he received his sight, and followed Jesus in the way.

Here we find Jesus and His disciples making their way to and through Jericho. During this time, Jesus is a hot commodity, miracles, signs and wonders were in full effect everywhere. The voice of His movement had echoed causing crowds to follow Him and flock to Him. Blind Bartimaeus sat by the highway begging, his condition had put him a very bad situation. Bartimaeus was limited from having a normal life but it did not dictate that he had no life. He could have stayed home moping, complaining and crying the blues because he was blind but he made the best out of a bad situation. You have got to strive for better instead of settling for whatever.

1. SEE THE NEED

> This man was blind but not dumb. He had sense enough to go where the help was instead of waiting on the help to come to him.
>
> Jericho was a prosperous town with good weather and was a definite spot to get financial support in that day. Bartimaeus

could not work and he knew the Jews considered it righteous to help the less fortunate. Yes, he was blind and could not see, but he could walk, talk and hear. Let me bless you when I say this! STOP FOCUSING ON WHAT YOU CAN'T DO AND START DOING YOUR BEST WITH WHAT YOU CAN DO. You have got to use what you got to get what you need. Verse 47 states that he heard that Jesus was close and he began to shout out "JESUS!!!!" Son Of David have mercy on me!" By him being in the situation he was in:

1. Bartimaeus could only go by what he heard.

2. Bartimaeus was illiterate to the law.

3. Bartimaeus was considered socially powerless.

Meaning, don't you let how you are viewed veto your victory. Your status is changing and I decree that your best is coming out of your bad situation. Often times people miss God all because they are playing into people's opinions of them. If you are going to truly make the best out a bad situation, you have to let people spectate and not dictate. Why? Because misery loves company and everybody that smiles at you is not smiling for you.

2. SEIZE THE OPPORTUNITY
   A. Bartimaeus knew he had nothing to lose.
   B. Bartimaeus was tired of being how he was.
   C. Bartimaeus recognized the Lords ability before ever experiencing it.

3. SERIOUS ABOUT A SOLUTION
   In verse 48, the people yelled at this blind man and told him to "SHUT UP!" The text suggest that he got even louder "Son of David, have mercy on me!!!" If you are going to Change Your Status you must:

   A. Keep people out of your ear, especially when your condition is exposed.

   B. Don't let people and their comments stop you from getting the Lord's attention.

   C. Don't Give Up!

You must believe and become totally convinced in the Lord's ability to perform whatever you need Him to perform. You almost have to go into a zone, blocking everything and everybody out to a point where the Lord totally consumes your purpose. Here is a moment of truth; you and I both know that considering the stuff you are dealing with right now that you don't have time to be gambling on people who need the Lord's help worse than you do. I challenge you to get serious about a solution NOW! So serious that you go after God regardless to what is being said about you or to you.

> Verse 49 Jesus heard Bartimaeus scream and holler, stopped and said "tell him to come here"
>
> Verse 50 Bartimaeus threw aside his coat and jumped up and came to Jesus. This would suggest that he left what he valued to go after what he needed.
>
> Verse 51 Jesus asked him "What do you want me to do for you?"
>
> ***Ephesians 3:20 Now unto Him that is able to do exceeding abundantly above all we could ask or think.***

The blind man said Lord "I want to see" He was specific about what he wanted the Lord to do for him.

Verse 52 Jesus said go thy way; thy faith has made thee whole. Immediately he recovered his sight and followed Jesus.

Changing your status puts you in the most powerful position you can ever experience in life, because at that very moment you take complete control of your current situation and open it up to the possibility of change and improvement. Don't allow opposition to blind you to opportunity. I speak prophetically through the pages of this book when I say this; "YOU DON'T HAVE TO STAY THERE!"

Chapter 6
LIVE BEYOND THE SHADOW OF DOUBT

Mark 11:23-24 (KJV)
²³ For verily I say unto you, That whosoever shall say unto this mountain, Be thou removed, and be thou cast into the sea; and shall not doubt in his heart, but shall believe that those things which he say shall come to pass; he shall have whatsoever he says.
²⁴ Therefore I say unto you, what things so ever ye desire, when ye pray, believe that ye receive them, and ye shall have them.

In many cases the people who suffer loss as a result of doubt, are people who have the ability to get it done but doubt keeps them stuck and stagnant.

Doubt does 3 things:

- **Stunts growth**
(NO EXCELLING/MATURING)
- **Kills momentum**
(ALWAYS STARTING AND STOPPING)
- **Limits Your Perception**
(ENSLAVES YOU TO RIGHT NOW)

Doubters are people who generally implement self-inflicted boundaries on themselves because their potential scares them. There mindset is " let me put up some boundaries, because I'm really comfortable with who I am and the anointed, powerful, unstoppable person on the inside of me might pull me out of the place that I've mastered". Doubt enslaves you to places that can't even accommodate what's on the inside of you. If you're going to live beyond the shadow of doubt, you can't be scared to speak to big things. In verse 23, Jesus told them to speak to the MOUNTAIN! I don't care how big, your situation is; I challenge you to speak to it in faith. If you are going to live beyond doubts, you cannot feel INFERIOR, INADEQUATE or INTIMIDATED. Yes to doubt = no to destiny. Why? Because you will never make it to a place that you're uncertain if it exists or will happen in your life.

Jesus said "whoever shall say to THIS Mountain be thou removed and be thou cast into the sea" which suggest that you must be specific and direct in removing anything that limits you in pursuing your destiny. This validates that you're changing your status by taking authority over your situation, but you can't stop there you must take authority over your flesh and feelings also. The text says "and shall not doubt in his heart, but shall believe"; because if you don't you will become a product of everybody else's ability and bound to your own inabilities. I challenge you to come out of your comfort zone by getting away from the things you're good at, familiar with and have done before. I declare that now is the time for you to stop basing your success on other people's accomplishments. Verse 23 explains that the mountain represent situations of impossibilities, which makes it safe to say that some situations you face in life should be spoke to and not prayed about. Now don't get me wrong, prayer is ALWAYS in order, but why pray about something that the Father has given you the answer to way before you opened your mouth. The magnitude of your manifestation depends on you believing the words you are speak out of your mouth.

I have been guilty of ignorantly having contradictory conversations; which means that I spoke things that drained the momentum of my destiny all because I was unaware at that time that WORDS HAVE POWER. Words are powerful and alive that we employ by giving them jobs they should not be assigned to. So the next time you find yourself in a discussion or conversation, make it your business to give your words the right assignment. Shifting correctly and succeeding continuously start and end with speaking the right words, because they are only going to produce what you assigned them to do.

Chapter 7
MASTER YOUR SEASON

1 Peter 1:6-7 (KJV)
⁶ Wherein ye greatly rejoice, though now for a season, if need be, ye are in heaviness through manifold temptations:
⁷ That the trial of your faith, being much more precious than of gold that perishes, though it be tried with fire, might be found unto praise and honor and glory at the appearing of Jesus Christ:

The word SEASON means "a **period of time when something is at its best or available; a period marked by certain conditions or activities suitable, proper, fitting, right and proper for that appointed time. (Webster)**

We have a variation of seasons that we generally experience depending on our region or demographics such as winter, spring, summer, and fall. Sometimes we experience what I like to call uncommon seasons such as Rainy, Dry, Storm and even The FLU season. Though they are all very different, yet there is one thing that is universal about them all, they are all periods of time marked by certain conditions and activities that are suitable, proper, fitting and right for what takes place in them. Ecclesiastes 3:1 says To EVERYTHING there is a season (Period of time where things are best & available).... We all know what a season is but many don't know WHAT season it is.

THREE VITAL KEYS TO MASTERING YOUR SEASON

1. Don't take a permanent position in a short season.

2. Understand certain things must happen in particular seasons.

3. Knowing where you are prepares your expectations.

This is important because too many believers are getting caught off guard not being prepared for a particular season. Why? Because they don't know what to look for.
Step 1 STAY HAPPY

In 1 Peter Verse 6, it starts by saying "Greatly rejoice" because of God's promises, we can truly be glad and experience a deep spiritual joy. This happiness remains unhindered and unchanged by what happens or takes place in your life.

Step 2 STAY PROGRESSIVE

Verse 6 continues by saying "Though now for a season". What you experience doesn't happen without a purpose, but despite the episodes currently going on in your life, God must be trusted to carry out HIS purposes in your life even during times of heavy trials or a severe season you don't understand. We must learn to accept these seasons as a part of the refiner's process and embrace the fact that this is how we grow.

Step 3 STAY POISED

Verse 7 "The trial of your faith (Testing)"... meaning it's designed to produce a certain result in and from our lives. God may very well have a different purpose for what we go through, but one thing is clear and universal about every trial is that it shows that our faith is strong and pure. But it takes the fire of trials, struggle and persecution to purify our faith. The Lord values fire-tested, stress-tested, and pressure-tested faith. The Lord endorses character assassinated faith, slandered name faith, insulted integrity faith, lied on faith and accusation tested faith. Through trials, the Lord burns away our self-reliance, self-sufficiency and self-serving attitudes. You must stay poised, assured, composed, balanced, steady, ready and prepared for action!

I Peter 4:12 Says "don't think it to be strange when fiery trials hit, because they are purposed to try you, as though some strange thing that is happening unto you". Don't act like it is something strange or foreign concerning what's happening to you. What you are going through is on an assignment to assist in the process of perfecting you. James 1:2 says to consider it a pleasure when you are tested. Verse 4 says" let patience have her perfect work in you". You never knew you had character until it was assassinated. You never knew you had integrity until your name was slandered. You never knew you had destiny until your purpose was attacked. **In actuality you should be shouting over the people that:**

Left you because it revealed who's with you

Lied on you because it revealed who's endorsing you.

Did you wrong because it revealed who has your back.

Used you because it revealed who supports you.

Everything that happens to you has purpose and potential wrapped in it.

Just because you have a:

Few bad hours doesn't mean you're going to have a bad day.

Few bad days doesn't mean you're going to have a bad month.

Few bad months doesn't mean you're going to have a bad year.

So what makes you think since you've fallen into diver's temptations, it has the ability to affect your season? God told me to tell you "It's still a good season; you're just experiencing some bad weather." You must understand that what you are going through is designed to develop your destiny. Once you fully understand and embrace where you are headed you'll appreciate where you are. People who break down when they go through where they are, generally don't plan on leaving where they are. So instead of seeing their trial as preparation for where they are going, they interpret the test as destruction to where they are staying. In conclusion, I want to encourage you to use every opposition as an opportunity for you to become the best the world has ever seen. Since where you are now is not where you are staying, I encourage you to move with holy boldness and get ready **to CHANGE YOUR STATUS!**

ABOUT THE AUTHOR

James D. Holiday Sr. started his journey in ministry on June 30, 1994 and since then has ministered on platforms throughout the United States and Africa. He is a Chicago native that holds a Bachelor's Degree in Christian Education and a Master's Degree in divinity. James is a devoted husband to Nicole A. Holiday and a devoted father to James Jr. and Nicholas. In September 2009, Pastor Holiday obeyed God's voice and organized Word of Change Christian Fellowship and since its inception has gained great momentum. Many miracles signs and wonders are being performed under his leadership at Word of Change, souls are being saved and lives are changed one word at a time. As an apostolic leader, he has raised up several sons & daughters in ministry that are relentless in establishing and advancing God's Kingdom. There is no doubt he is an anointed preacher & teacher of the word and has a strong Apostolic/Prophetic grace on his life to declare present truth; his passion for the things of God fuel his efforts to advance, establish and pioneer in this season.

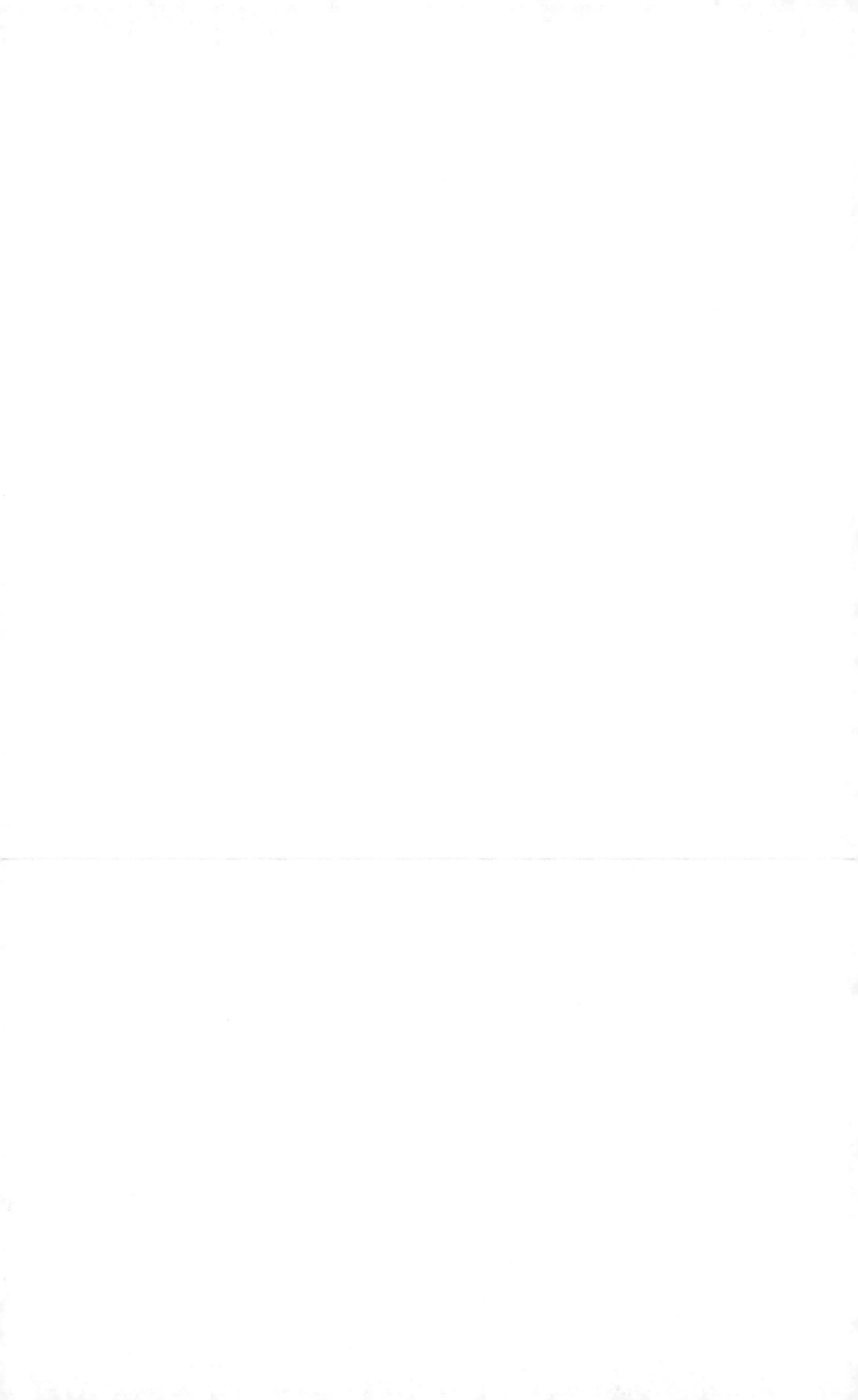

www.ingramcontent.com/pod-product-compliance
Lightning Source LLC
LaVergne TN
LVHW021622080426
835510LV00019B/2727